Ancient Egyptian Rhyme Time

Illustrations by Shannon Milsom.
Cover by Suellen Peskett.
Thanks to Corinne Lawrence for feedback and editing.

About The Author

Shirley is a poet and author of children's books. Her poems have been published in a wide range of magazines and anthologies, and have won or been placed in a number of competitions.

Shirley lived in Egypt for a while. She was fascinated by its history and visited many of its historical monuments.

She has been a teacher for many years and uses poetry in her classes to make learning fun and develop literacy skills. This is her first poetry collection for children.

Find out more about her poems and books here.
https://shirleyannecook.wordpress.com/
https://shirleyharberauthor.wordpress.com/

Email: shirmemo@aol.com

Contents

An ABC Of Ancient Egypt

A is for Akhet, season of flood,
B is for beer that Egyptians loved.
C is for croc, the aquatic reptile,
D is for delta at the mouth of the Nile.
E's for embalming - a mummy was made,
F is for fan - keeping cool in the shade.

G is for Giza, where the pyramids stand,
H is for Hittites, who tried to steal land.
I is for incense, often worn on the head,
J is for jackal, symbol of the dead.

1

K is for Karnak, temple of Amun,

L is for labyrinth that stood in Faiyum.

M is for Meritaten, an Egyptian queen,

N's for natron that would keep your clothes clean.

O is for obelisk, a column so tall,

P is for paintings adorning the wall.

Q is for quarry, where limestone was found,

R's for Rosetta, a stone to astound.

S is for scribes, who recorded everything,

T is for Tut - the famous boy King.

U's for uraeus, marked out as divine,

V is for vizier, ministers of the time.

W's for wab priest, in his fine linen gown,

X is for Xois - an old Egyptian town.

Y is for Yuya, buried with his jars,

Z is for zodiac, Egyptians loved stars.

Cinquains

Amun

King of the gods
Father of the
pharaohs
Combines with
sun god Amun-
Ra.
Hidden One

Horus

Falcon-headed
The pharaoh's
protector
Son of Isis and Osiris
Sky god

Hathor

Divine goddess
of dance, music
and love
Sacred mother of
the pharaohs
Cow god

An Egyptian Child's Present List

I'd like a ball made of papyrus,
a wooden spinning top,
and a really cool rattle
like my mate Seti's got.
But what I want oh, so much more,
is a wooden crocodile
with a moving jaw!

The Secret Of The Nile

I am born
high in hills.
Trickle, at first,
then, a tumultuous gush
as rocks quake beneath
my rumbling, tumbling rush.
A pause as I lingeringly kiss
white waters, then flow onwards
with my precious gift.

You, Egyptian farmers,
await my annual flood,
to plant seeds in my
rich black blood.
I watch you toil,
as I slither past,
and breath in sweet scents
of Nile grass.

Your kings find
eternal rest in tombs
built upon my banks.
I hear priests chanting
songs to the gods
as they give thanks,
while women in white,
diaphanous dresses
shed tears into
my sapphire depths.

I have also cradled
prophets in my papyrus bed,
and on those pressed stems
their stories will be read.
But remember, Egyptians,
as I journey to the sea,
if not for my flow you
would have no history.
Your kings may be wise
and rule a long while,
but they do not know
where I begin,
my secret of the Nile.

Limericks

There was once a man called Tut,
whose chariot got stuck in a rut.
He said, 'What a curse!
Could my life be worse?
I've broken my tooth on a nut!'

There was a man called Ahmose,
who had rather large toes.
No sandals would fit –
he didn't like it one bit
as he was ridiculed by his Hittite foes.

Rameses Rap

As pharaohs go, man, you were great
'cos a long rule was to be your fate.
Sixty-six years spent on the throne:
your name recorded forever on stone.

Rameses, Rameses, super king,
ninety-six wives and lots of bling.
Rameses, Rameses, what a cool dude –
one hundred children is quite a brood.

A brave warrior, you fought many foes,
and did it well, so the story goes.
At Kadesh you battled against cranky Hittites,
in one of your most famous fights.
A temple wall depicts the win:
some said it was a pretty close thing.
The treaty – signed – meant a peaceful rule –
the first in history, wasn't that cool?

Rameses, Rameses super king
ninety-six wives and lots of bling.
Rameses, Rameses, what a cool dude
two hundred children is quite a brood.

You erected many monuments sublime,
most of which stand the test of time.
Huge statues of you shone in the light.
They were built to show your godly might.
Stunning tombs made for your queens –
there was no end to your building schemes.
People prospered under your reign:
when you died Egypt was not the same.

Rameses, Rameses super king,
ninety-six wives and lots of bling.
Rameses, Rameses, what a cool dude,
One hundred children is quite a brood.

Anubis

I lurk in the shadows,
waiting for your death.
I am Anubis,
jackal-headed god
of the afterlife
and mummification,
protector of graves
and cemeteries.

When you die I will take you
to stand before Osiris.
Your heart will be
balanced on the scales
against the feather of Ma'at.

If you have lived a bad life
and your heart sinks
it will be devoured by Ammit.
So lead a good life and you will rise to paradise.

Rameses II (A Kenning)

Chariot racer

Loving partner

Prolific father

Fearless commander

Wise leader

Skilful archer

City founder

Peace maker

God worshiper

Festival planner

Monument builder

Extensive trader

Lion lover

Great ruler

The Mask Of Tutankhamen

I have fashioned his funerary mask
from the flesh of the gods –
burnished and beaten,
it shines like the sun-god Ra.
He has eyes made of white quartz
and black obsidian –
lids, brows and kohl marks
are precious lapis-lazuli.
The full lips and fine chin,
make it a true likeness of the boy king.

The royal nemes headdress
is solid gold with stripes of blue paste glass,
finished in a lapis and gold plait.
Nekhbet and Wadjet adorn the brow.
They will dazzle the underworld.

I have created a masterpiece.
But no man will ever see its beauty.
soon it will be entombed
for eternity.

The Discovery

Highclere Castle 1922:
Dear Howard,
I have funded your search for years:
sadly, this must be the last season,
my finances are in arrears.

Egypt 1922:
My dear George.
Thank you. Please send the money soon.
I am sure that in the next few days
I will locate Tut's tomb.

Highclere Castle 1922:
Dear Howard,
I hope so, as you deserve
a fitting end to your long quest.
And old chap, you're probably in need
of a very good rest!
Egypt 1922:
Dear George,
No time to rest, I am combing the area,

I have a grid system in place.
As the young folk might say –
Watch this space!

Highclere Castle 1922:
Dear Howard,
Well I wish you luck then,
my dear old friend.
My fingers are crossed for
a truly successful end.
Telegram from Carter to Lord Carnarvon

Egypt November 5th 1922:
'Have found the entrance to Tut's tomb!
Seals intact. You'd better get here very, very soon.'

Telegram from Lord Carnarvon to Carter Highclere
November 5th:
Such spiffing news! I am on the way.
This is a truly momentous day!

NB. Travelling back then was not easy.
It took Carnarvon two weeks to get to Egypt,
travelling by ship, train, ship, train then a donkey
ride.
Carter must have been going bananas
as he waited to look inside!

Hatshepsut: Queen Of Egypt

Hatshepsut, born in 1508 BC,
was the first great woman of history.
The grieving widow of King Thutmose,
she took his throne, (and all his clothes!)
and ruled from 1478 BC.
Amun, she said, was her authority.

Reigning over them all for twenty years,
Egypt lived happily with no fears.
The all-powerful Pharaoh in her day
got to do things just her way.
She traded briskly with many countries,
introducing ebony, gold and trees,
frankincense, and other fragrant spices –
was unafraid to haggle over prices.
Egyptians prospered during her time,
but then her heir committed the crime
of deleting her name from the dynasty,
which doesn't say much for his honesty!
But monuments bear witness to her name,
so we today know of her fame.

The story Of Osiris And Seth.

So long ago, in Egypt,
god Osiris sat on the throne
but brother Seth was jealous,
and wanted it for his own.

He made a golden chest,
just his brother's size
and said, 'Whomsoever this fits
will have it as a prize.'
Lots of people came to try.

Some were far too tall.
Others had hair that was too
thick
Many couldn't get in at all.

Of course, when Osiris tried it,
the box was a perfect fit.
Then Seth slammed down the lid.
He didn't care one bit.
He threw the chest into the Nile,

and watched poor Osiris drown.
He was so triumphant
for now he had the crown.

God Isis, wife of Osiris,
searched high and low for the chest.
Finding it far away in Byblos,
she sat down for a rest.

But as she slept there in the shade
Seth came by that day,
recognized the chest he'd made,
stole Osiris's body away.
He chopped it into pieces
which he scattered over the earth,
but Isis gathered them up
for Anubis to give them rebirth.

Now in the underworld,
Osiris could not be with his wife.
Ra put him in charge of the dead,
so he ruled the afterlife.

Each year on the Nile bank
sad Isis sits and cries.
Many still believe that her tears
Make the river waters rise.

Being A Scarab Beetle.

It isn't exactly my idea of fun,
pushing around a ball of dung.
As if that's not bad enough
I even have to eat the stuff!
But Egyptians revere - surprisingly -
scarab beetles just like me.
It's a symbol of rebirth, you see,
and so I am called 'Khepri'.

Egyptians like a scarab charm
to keep them safe from any harm.
And that's so special, don't you think?
So does it really matter if I stink?

Ancient Gardeners

Sirius glitters in the night sky
and heralds Akhet,
the season of the Nile flood.
Soon the banks will overflow
with rich black silt – Egypt's life blood.

When the waters recede
farmers will plough the ground,
while women and children
scatter seed around.
This season of sowing they call Peret.

Shemu, harvest time, comes next.
Bronze backs will glisten
and sickles flash in sun god Ra's harsh rays.
When the granaries are full,
everyone will sing Amun's praise.

On the tomb walls of Set Maat,
artists record this seasonal story.
The ancient gardener's world,
there for eternity.

Dreaming Of Tut

He comes to me in blue and gold:
is such a wonder to behold.
So handsome in a regal gown
and on his head the double crown.

He tells me he's the new boy king,
and proudly waves the royal ring.
Asks if I want to see his land,
'It's more than pyramids and sand.'

In his barge we cruise The Nile,
steer past a fearsome crocodile.
But I have never known such heat –
I'm thankful we've a shaded seat.
The people wave as we pass by,
'Long live the pharaoh!' they all cry.

Soon we sail into a lake.
I gasp and do a double take.
For standing tall and shining white,
an awesome view comes into sight.

His palace stretches far and wide,
and I can't wait to see inside.

We disembark: he shows me round
where there's so much to be found
from frescoed walls and marbled floors
to inlaid caskets, chests and doors.

I'm ushered to a golden chair
as servants scurry everywhere:
serve plates of roasted duck and quail
and cups of juices, wine and ale.

Musicians play a soft refrain
as palace dancers entertain.
The smell of incense fills the air
and petals are strewn everywhere.

After lunch we take a stroll:
the palace guards are on patrol.
We walk by palms, a deep blue pool,
and temple walls where air is cool.

Then Tut asks me to be his queen.
I wake up. It was all a dream!

Pyramids!

The first pyramid (its sides like steps),
was sixty metres high.
Egyptians believed their king could climb
to the sun god in the sky.

Later pyramids' sides were flat —
the earth shown as a mound.
Egyptians thought the world began
by pushing through watery ground.

The Great Pyramid of Pharaoh Khufu
is very, very tall.
If you stood right next to it,
you'd look extremely small!

It's constructed of two million stones
weighed in two tonne blocks,
I've always wondered how they managed
to move such very large rocks?

Dark and secret chambers formed
the pharaohs' pyramid tombs:
essentials for the afterlife
were packed in hidden rooms.
Built this way, Egyptians thought
to safeguard all their treasures:
but this was very far from true –
thieves just ignored these measures.

Heavy bolts and seals on rooms
left few burglars perplexed.
Since awful curses did not work
the viziers were really vexed.

Nothing seemed to work at all:
crooks managed still to thrive:
the guilty were punished horribly –
impaled or burnt alive.

They still had problems even then,
(it seems a bit unfair)
the death sentence meant no afterlife –
so executions were rare!

Making Papyrus

Cut the papyrus stem
into pieces of equal length,
and peel away the outer fibres.
Slice the inner core
into thin strips
and lay several
alongside each other.

Place another set
of papyrus strips
at right angles to the first.
Moisten then firmly beat together.
Leave under a heavy stone to dry.

Then using a flat stone
polish the papyrus sheet
to a smooth sheen.
Trim the edges.
Glue the sheets together
to make a scroll.
Write a letter to the pharaoh and his queen!

Apprentice

I gaze at the gold sweepings
pooling in the crucible,
a swirling sunset dances before my eyes.
I breathe in the scent of metal
wipe the sweat from my brow,
then pour the molten liquid
into the hollowed stone.
The bright reds and yellows fade
as it cools and hardens,
with no trace of a blemish.

I spend my days, fashioning
ingots from the flesh of the gods.
One day I will be a master goldsmith
and wondrous objects will spring
from my fingertips:
golden pectorals to adorn noblemen's chests,
necklaces to caress Princesses' soft necks
and my master piece - a funerary mask.
It will shine like the sun god Ra
and gild a Pharaoh's face for eternity.

Egyptian Flood Rap

Let us thank Hapi for the inundation.
Soon we'll have lots of vegetation.
Oh what a super situation!
For there won't be any more starvation.

Let us all sing and clap our hands.
Egypt's one of the greatest lands!

We will have such a celebration
as we begin the germination.
The scribes will make the evaluation.
But please don't take too much taxation!

Let us all sing and clap our hands -
Egypt's one of the greatest lands.

Rameses is cool at administration,
So let us show our gratification.
We will all have a great vacation.
Come on and sing an incantation!

Let us all sing and clap our hands
Egypt's one of the greatest lands.

Shape Poem

```
N
 I
  L
   O
    M
     E
      T
       E
        R
```

A step-like stone structure,
leading down into the river.
Priests used it to measure   Too high,
devastation!
the level of the Nile flood water.   Too low,
no vegetation.

An 'Inside' Poem

Inside the pyramid is a tomb.

Inside the tomb is a room.

Inside the room is a canopic jar.

Inside the jar is a piece of linen.

Inside the linen is an embalmed stomach.

It once was inside a famous monarch!

King Tut's Burial

(Another 'Inside' poem)

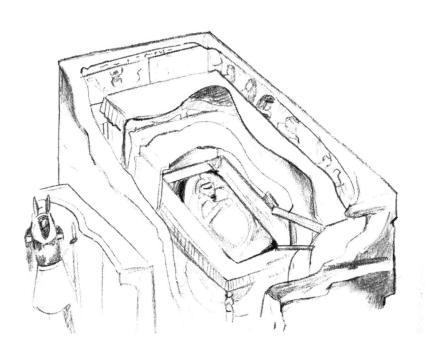

Inside the outer shrine is a linen pall.

Inside the pall is a second shrine.

Inside is a third shrine.

Inside is the inner shrine.

Inside is a granite sarcophagus.

Inside is a coffin.

Inside is a second coffin.

Inside is a third coffin.

Inside is a funerary mask.

Inside is the mummy of King Tut!

So many coffins and shrines! Well he was divine!

Diary Of An Apprentice Scribe

Monday, hieroglyphs to write.
Thanks, Thoth! I got them all right!
Tuesday, history today, then
back to the hieroglyphics again,
before working on my cursive writing.
Got told off (me and Seti were fighting)
Wednesday, prayed in the temple a while,
then messed about with Seti by the Nile.
Thursday, lessons on maths and law –
Yawn, yawn – I found them such a bore.
Friday, had to translate a classical text:
it left me feeling rather vexed.
Saturday, a poem to learn and recite:
It took me nearly all the night.
Sunday, a day out with Dad and Mum –
We sailed to Thebes, had such fun.

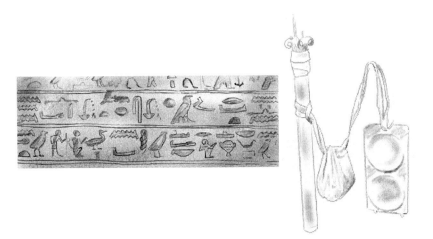

The Nile

The water of the Nile shimmers
stirred by a gentle breeze.
A small boy splashes happily:
a mother washes on her knees.

A young man works a shaduf,
as his forebears did long ago.
He gives thanks for this river,
praising 'Happi' for the flow.

In hazy heat a dog is sleeping,
above a rotating horde of flies.
From the reeds an ibis rises,
a flash of white in azure skies.

Now a boat breaks the waters,
from Aswan a load of stone,
is bound for the Pharaoh's palace
to make statues and a throne.

Epitaphs

Here lies the body
of dear Ahmose.
How he died no one knows!

In memory of Cleo
my pet crocodile,
who was eaten by a hippo
in the Nile.

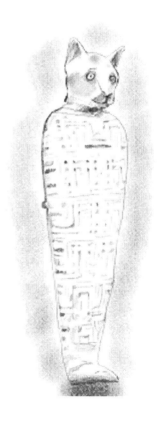

In this tomb
lies the body
of Tut's nurse.
Don't touch anything,
there's a curse!

Here lies my beloved cat,
Amun.
She was taken from me
far too soon.

Printed in Poland
by Amazon Fulfillment
Poland Sp. z o.o., Wrocław

50657692R00031